This publication is dedicated to

"To those I learn the most from":
Karen Errigo, my Mother;
John J. Errigo, Jr., my father;
Marlene Errigo, my Aunt;
John J. Taylor, my Grandfather;
Laura M. Martinetti;
Alejandro G. Gonzalez and
"All those who want to make their **Big Idea** to the global stage!"


Special Thanks to Gerard E. Mayers,


**Made and Printed in the USA**

Mention of specific companies, organizations, or authorities in this book does not imply endorsement by the publisher, not does the mention of specific companies, organizations, or authorities imply that they endorse this book.

Copyright © 2011 by Holistic Organizational Development and Training, Inc.®,
and Quincentennial Publishing Company
All rights, including the right to reproduce this booklet or any portion thereof in any form, whether print, electronic, audio, or for motion pictures or television, are reserved.

Published by Green Oak Press, LLC

HODT Inc.®, and Holistic Organizational Development and Training, Inc.®
are registered trademarks and may not be used in commerce.

Printed/Published in the United States of America

Cover Art designed by Award Winning

ISBN 978-1940927046

Library of Congress Control Number: 2011930533

Any questions or comments?

Please send request via e-mail or to write to the author at:

John@JohnErrigo.com

Green Oak Press

**EDITION**

Winter 2014

12345678812414

www.greenoakpress.com

PO BOX 6756

Lawrenceville, NJ 08648

## Contents

Marketing Transformed into a Lean Revolution ............................ 8

How Marketing Revolutionizes as A Big Idea! ............................ 10

Marketing Research: ................................................................. 14

Ask Bigger Questions than "Would You Like a Coffee with that?"
..................................................................................................... 14

The Theory behind Asking the Big Questions ............................ 18

I Think that Person Over There is a Big Fan of the Beatles?! ..... 20

The Theory behind Marketing Segmentation ............................ 21

A Plan to Sell a Product to a Certain Person: Results 99.9% Guaranteed! ................................................................................ 23

    A Marketing Model Summary ............................................. 26

Would You Rather a Blueberry Pie or Just Some ........................ 27

Blueberries & Ice Cream? ........................................................... 27

Big Questions, Big Answers! How about Playing ....................... 29

"Who Wants to be a Millionaire?" .............................................. 29

Smart Begets Smart ..................................................................... 30

Social Media Marketing "A Force of Nature" .............................. 32

The Force behind Marketing: What Drives Results? ................... 37

Being Ethical Is Smart Strategy and Financially Rewarding ........ 39

Starting the Revolution of Your "Big Idea" .................................. 43

Index of Sources .......................................................................... 45

## Marketing Transformed into a Lean Revolution

You have an idea! It is imagined as the next best thing. Already you see the success and financial gains of your brilliance. A new home in LA would be nice; how about a second home in Maine? You start planning the material success with the luxuries of these mansions. How about an in-home movie theater equipped with a custom made Italian marble Jacuzzi? Immediately you start putting money behind this idea since you believe in it so strongly. Calls are being made to your friends and family about this masterpiece. The rush of being hyped and pumped start running through your veins and then you start to put the brilliant idea in action. You even consult a few close advisors and they are excited too. Not to be a naysayer, but there is something tragically missing from your brilliant inspiration. Your creative idea *is already set to fail*. It failed before it even had a chance. Why? Simple. Any initiative implemented without a solid marketing plan before anything else is running down an unsustainable path. It is on the path to being nothing more than just a creative stroke of genius and sadly, a missed opportunity. There is an old saying that is still true: *If you fail to plan, you plan to fail!*

More than ever, effective marketing has the tremendous power to develop and transform a great idea into something really big. With the dawn of our information age to the present, word of mouth spreads faster than ever. A single tweet can set the stage of a presidential candidacy; it can announce a new relationship; and launch a brand new product. All of these messages have the power to change a person's life within a matter of minutes. Before you can even fathom the impact of your tweet, it has been carried around the world in mere seconds. A key message is known, via the speed of light, instantly. A good example is Apple Inc.'s original announcement of its new product, the iPad. Right after the announcement of this innovative product, people were literally sending tweets at the rate of thousands per second about the new technology. People were crazy about this new technology before anyone really knew all the details of the product. We can glean from this example a powerful marketing lesson. The power of the message carries faster than time itself. If you combine the solid marketing techniques of the past with the power of almost instant messaging, just think how revolutionary the marketing of your idea can become…today! Marketing, however, needs to be the first and foremost principle of action behind any great idea.

Long gone are times of combing through 600 page books and multiple series on the topic of marketing; those pages and series take too long to lay out the principles in detail and to digest them. This learning method is outdated. *Today* is the start of a new method. This single booklet of 64 pages will provide the same basic marketing principles and give you a foundation to quickly apply a new strategy in the same amount of time it takes to send a message via the social media forums. This booklet will start you on the path to a new and simpler transformation without losing the timeless principles needed to teach any novice or experienced professional alike. Welcome to the Lean Marketing Revolution.

## How Marketing Revolutionizes as A Big Idea!

Have you ever been somewhere and noticed; this business is really doing well?! This thought occurs to me at each visit to Starbucks. They have everything; little tiny 180 calorie cupcakes at the cost of a mere $1.59 including tax. The calories seem just right and so does the price; however the cupcake is really small. The green-tea latte which is my favorite is also a bit pricey and so are the other desserts and food on display. Despite all this, the place is packed and one of my favorites to visit. There is nothing unique about the shops; they are pretty much the same; they are ubiquitous; the coffee is definitely different but my conclusion of why they are so busy is the way the barista treats me. You feel important when you are at Starbucks; it is an experience. Their marketing strategy begins and ends with the experience. They want you to have an amazing experience while you are in the store. The CEO of Starbucks made certain the aroma from the coffee beans returned to their pre-1990 levels since it was being overtaken by breakfast sandwiches and other specialty items. It was important to the CEO of Starbucks to have the aroma of coffee literally wafting from his stores. After all, it *is* a coffee shop.

The topic of marketing is changing dramatically from the product to being about the experience. Even opening a can of Coca-Cola (or any other soft drink) and drinking the refreshing beverage is an experience. Think of your favorite place to shop, or your favorite place to have a beer, why did you decide to go there? What makes this place so unique? Ask yourself this question about your current business. What makes it unique? Is it the people you have working for you, or is it the people you work for? What about the product? Has the company you have worked for built a brand for over 100 years, or are you a new company? What do you see your company doing in ten years? Hopefully it will continue to make a lot of money; without having something unique your business might not survive in today's viral and "now" market. Today, the experience for the customer is just as important as the product itself. The product often times creates the experience and vice versa.

One success about experience marketing goes back to the potato chip. Back in the first days of production, the folks who made the first potato chip were worried that it would not sell, since it tasted so much better right when it was hot, fresh from production than a few hours later after it cooled down. The unique potato chip, which tasted better hot, was now going to be packaged into a bag and sold. Nobody who tried the hot chips thought this would be a success. If you ask anyone today what is their favorite potato chip, you bet, someone will have an answer.

They will have an immediate answer at best. Think of your favorite potato chip, why is *this* chip your favorite? There was some magical thinking long ago about how to create a potato chip that even after it cools it would be a sensation. This magical thinking was marketing and these same marketing principles that applied back then still apply today. The potato chip was something unique all by itself and this may be the reason for its success. It was unique and created an experience.

Uniqueness is exactly what we are aiming for today in our marketing revolution. Think of something unique; but you also have to think outside the box. Marketing has been around for a long time and has been a topic of interest at least since the first product/service was created and sold. The field gained momentum in the 1950's when it was seen as a subject of interest to companies and academia. How did Henry Ford become the most successful salesman in the 20$^{th}$ Century? Did he study a Marketing course at Harvard? No. He had instinctive skills and business knowledge which helped him on his way. He once commented that the biggest success for any business is to keep swinging the door open in the morning. Although this is good advice, it has modest value in regards to marketing. Marketing is much more than opening the door in the morning; however, the principle of hard work still applies today as well as tomorrow.

How to market your next big idea is waiting just around the corner and this book will get you thinking about how to get *your* big idea out of your mind and into action. No idea has worth unless it can be sold. Let me say it a bit differently: Ideas help get to the big picture; to make an idea worth money, it has to be something which can be sold, packaged and delivered. Marketing is the only way this can be done.

Anyone who has visited Times Square in New York City notices the value of marketing. Who decided to put up these vast and expensive posters surrounded by bright lights? This was not done by accident; it was rather a deliberate choice made by a team of marketing professionals who developed a solid strategy based upon their research, which led them to know who the audience is and who would be best walking around the bright spot in New York City seeking out their advertisement. It is an expensive choice; however, the marketing team is betting this choice will be a good investment. How it will provide an investment would also be a part of a marketing strategy. Does the company seek brand recognition, or is there a local shop around the corner which the marketing strategy was designed to entice shoppers. There is a broad method and strategy chosen for the bright flashy billboards in New York City on display peering down upon you as you walk around the cornered streets. Put otherwise, this concept is known in business and in marketing as a Return on Investment (ROI) and can be a powerful tool in both marketing analysis and research. It can also help define or re-define an organization's marketing strategy. If the big flashy ad in Times Square did not create the objectives it was meant to create, then the marketing plan *failed*.

In beginning stages of forming a marketing strategy, there must be a methodology to guide the plan. As fancy at it might sound, a marketing methodology is as simple as asking a bunch of questions, but more importantly the *right* questions. When you go to your favorite place, think for a minute, why do you go there? Go back to my Starbucks example. The experience is my answer; even though it is pricey, nobody beats their customer service. There is nothing innovative about selling coffee; however it is the *way* it is sold. It is the way it is packaged and the way it carries a resonating message of helping farmers grow co-ops in Africa and other developing nations. Their message and way of service reverberates with so many people; they asked the right questions and the right people answered them. They bought a cup of coffee and a little cupcake as well.

## Marketing Research:

## Ask Bigger Questions than "Would You Like a Coffee with That?"

You have to ask yourself the right questions. If you look at marketing research and the two types of measurement of the questions being asked; quantitative and qualitative you will be on the right path in developing your strategy. These two methods sound difficult; however, they are quite simple. *Qualitative research* is the simplest form of marketing research. Think of getting yourself a new home, and you want to paint the house, you pick out a few colors and ask yourself a few questions. Before long, you walk out with the right colors which will complement your new home. The only problem is you are not exactly sure how the colors will look on your wall, and only when you paint the room will you know for sure. These same types of conclusions are drawn from qualitative research. Once you paint the color, you will still see variations of the color depending upon the type of weather. On sunny days the shade of jade will be bright green and on rainy days the same shade will be deep blue. The questions in qualitative research are preliminary at best, "I like that color jade but I am not sure how it will look in my room." And these questions are not as exact and therefore you will not get exact answers; you get conclusions.

Now in *quantitative research* it is more complex; exact questions are asked and you get exact answers. Suppose you want to market a new brand of towels, and you wanted to know what color would be most popular. You can have a few people in your family pick their favorite color and this would be the beginning of your quantitative research questioning process. All your answers will be different; you still need more information. The only way you will get the right and bigger answers is going after the big questions. Maybe the color of the towel is not as important as the feel of the towel. Perhaps the orange towel is the preference; a towel with a light peach color is the one ultimately bought because it feels softer and looks fancier. The questions in order to get this marketing strategy down are more complex. Perhaps the orange towels sell big in some areas of the country then others, and perhaps the softer and heavier towels sell better in colder climates. What type of material, texture, color, demographic, culture, and climate are examples of the exact kind of questions you would ask during quantitative research. They are exact and you will get exact answers.

Step back and look at the type of research (questions) you have decided upon; will they get the right answers and drive the results you want? Again, is the outcome brand recognition where someone will say, for example, "Oh, Apple, I know about them, they make fancy iPods," or is the intent for a customer to say, "Oh, Whole Foods, they are around the corner, I am going to stop in and get some fresh organic produce." It is the intent of marketers to drive a consumer to action and the how and why, and the end result of what the customer did. Did the customer recognize Apple, Inc. as the leading brand of high technology in the brand recognition strategy in posting a billboard in Times Square? Did a person take a walk by Whole Foods to buy the fresh produce which was seen in an article in the *New York Times*? What is the intent and what happens as a result of the consumer's actions are the two key questions when developing a marketing research strategy.

As we know from our example of the Times Square marketing strategy, the marketing team chose a big billboard ad to create brand recognition of Apple, Inc. For an illustrative example, a big Apple was hung right in the center of Times Square with bright dashing lights surrounding it. Now we have a slight dilemma. The marketing team needs to know how to measure if this marketing strategy was successful. Did the big flashy billboard work? How do we know if it created brand recognition? In order to know how well your marketing strategy worked, you have to decide upon a similar research method to measure the success. Marketing research and measurement (qualitative and quantitative methods) work hand-in-hand. These marketing research (questions) and measurement methods are intimately tied together. This is best done before executing the marketing strategy. There are two very important styles of measurement and they produce different results. "There is evidence within those who study marketing which suggest different measurement scales and measurement methodologies do in fact lead to different research outcomes."[1] As we have explored, the two traditional and essential marketing measurements include qualitative and quantitative marketing research methods.

Social media marketing (which will be explored later) is built upon the same strategies mentioned; however, the main point of social media marketing is *networking*. To build an online

---

[1] Robertshaw, 2007, p. 5

presence that is both easily assessable, useable *and* which creates brand recognition. In the subheading of Social Media Marketing, the LinkedIn example will provide more context into the social aspects of marketing and how it has literally changed the way we not only think about marketing but how much more abundant these very principles are.

## The Theory behind Asking the Big Questions

Quantitative marketing is about data, facts, information, and knowledge. Within the context of economic development, quantitative marketing focuses on business attraction strategies, processes and competencies that quantify and communicate a region's comparative advantage to individual firms.[2] Choosing a quantitative marketing methodology is the most specific and the most tedious. It uses very precise data to determine the target market of individual firms, developing the marketing message which is company-specific and what firms are essential to build relationships.[3] These are a lot of areas being measured. In marketing a quantitative method is much more scientific and much more complex than a qualitative method.

In deciding to use quantitative methodology, it also important to know how this information will be used. This methodology may not be appropriate for every firm "since no two

---

[2] Peterson, 2010
[3] Ibid.

operations are exactly alike, quantitative marketing is an individualized, highly targeted process."[4] The most important question to answer in developing an appropriate method is "What are you trying to do? What do you want to measure? What method will be best utilized to get the marketing questions answered?" For example, do you want to measure how many males bought a pair of driving gloves, what was their income bracket, how many purchased these gloves on credit or paid cash, and what part of the country did they live in. These types of detailed questions would be best served by using a quantitative research method of measurement.

Qualitative marketing measurement, often regarded as scientific and subjective may be less reliable since it does not collect all the facts as contained with quantitative methods. You may only get a handful of facts; but rather, a bunch of conclusions: Perhaps Johnny did go to Whole Foods Market since he saw the big ad in Times Square; this ad had a college student who appeared fit and wearing the latest workout clothes, and we noticed a lot of college students have been shopping at Whole Foods lately since we posted our ad in Times Square. This would be an informal way of how qualitative marketing would be measured. It is highly subjective and draws conclusions.

---

[4] Op. cit., p.36

Although qualitative marketing may seem more abstract than and not as black and white as quantitative marketing methodology, it does have its merits.

## I Think that Person Over There is a Big Fan of the Beatles?!

Think about it, you are out with a few friends at a concert. You notice some people are wearing Beatles shirts and some are wearing Rolling Stones shirts. You also notice a few people who are wearing Grateful Dead shirts too. How do you know? You have the evidence; you have observed them wearing these different shirts. It would be safe to assume that those people who are wearing the Beatles shirts like the Beatles, and those wearing the Rolling Stones shirts like the Stones. This simple observation is what makes a big part of marketing theory called segmentation. Marketing segmentation is really looking at patterns or information to make a conclusion. In the example of those who wear a certain band shirt, you are making a conclusion based upon information you have observed. While marketing segmentation is very complex, it should not be as hard as making an observation, getting the right information and then making a decision. It would probably be safe to go to someone wearing a Beatles shirt and ask them if they would like to buy a John Lennon Jacket versus going over to someone from the Grateful Dead crowd and trying to sell them the same jacket. You could sell the jackets to the two different types of people and be surprised; however your bet would be on the Beatles fan first. This is the same type of information marketing segmentation tries to obtain.

## The Theory behind Marketing Segmentation

Once a good marketing research method has been chosen in developing a marketing strategy, it is very important to move to the next phase of marketing planning: setting goals. Setting goals helps you in developing marketing segmentation, which is the most difficult aspect of the marketing process.

Marketing Segmentation is putting together a unique plan targeting those to whom you are going to market and how it will shape, flex and add value to the marketing strategy chosen. What does the fancy word Marketing Segmentation mean? Think again of walking through Times Square on a nice summer night in New York City, and as you look at the billboard ads there all sparkling and blinking, you notice many different types of ads. You notice which ads are for shoes, sporting events, concerts; you notice ads which may appeal to your significant other; and you may notice an ad which your aunt would enjoy, since she is a golfer. This is a good analogy of what marketing segmentation is; it is directly classifying your customers and whom you should market too. Just think of those ads again in Times Square. Only certain ads appealed to you; the same kind of mind set is needed in developing marketing segmentation.

Market segmentation is not simplistic. According to Tonks, who has studied marketing segmentation and has done scholarly research on the topic, segmentation theory is approached generally from a managerial perspective using the foundational elements of competitive and diverse markets, a financial impetus, a strategic and operational purpose and the affective priority given to customer satisfaction and using this data as a science. [5]

"The scientific approach to market segmentation was certainly prevalent in the 1960's and 1970's, coinciding with more normal approaches to marketing more generally."[6] Thinking only like a scientist may not work in the 21st Century. Today, you have to think outside the box. Think of the many clever advertising campaigns. You have dogs driving cars chasing cats; you have talking lizards and ducks; you have hamsters driving cool-looking cross-over vehicles; and other thinking outside the box ads. This is what works in the 21st century. These marketing plans were not meant only to attract other people who think outside the box; they were meant to attract a diverse market, people who may laugh and remember their spokesperson or slogan. Remember also that the success or failure of your marketing campaign for that entire year might hinge on whether your "outside the box" ad was viewed in a positive or negative light. What your target audience perceives is as, or more, important than your actual facts. Welcome to the new

---

[5] Tonks, 2009
[6] Tonks, 2009, p. 349

marketing model of doing business. Based upon the marketing research method chosen (quantitative or qualitative), you would be able to determine the success and failure of your marketing campaign.

## A Plan to Sell a Product to a Certain Person: Results 99.9% Guaranteed!

Market segmentation is concerned with classification of customers and answering questions regarding who would buy what, and what would happen if they do, would they like it and will they keep buying it over and over? For example, one such question might be "what types of people like tennis shoes"? The answer obviously is people who play tennis, but what income bracket of people are you marketing your tennis shoes to, are you looking to market a more expensive shoe, or an economical shoe, and are you focusing on a shoe for men or for women, what age group would you market to? These questions again will be answered by marketing segmentation research. "Conceptually, market segmentation can be defined as the process of subdividing a market into distinct subsets of customers that behave in the same way or have similar needs."[7] If the right questions are asked with a proper research and measurement method chosen, then you will have hit the ball out of the park. You have created a smart strategy which will get smart results!

---

[7] Foedermayr & Diamantopoulos, 2008, p. 223

In a hypothetical example, you found in your segmentation process that tennis may be a niche market for those in college, so your marketing segmentation research will focus on college students. You also found in your research more women play tennis than men; it would be smart to make your shoes attractive to the women who would buy them, and they would be reasonably priced since they are going to be bought by college students. These are key questions you would ask in the marketing segmentation process; once you get the answers as mentioned in the hypothetical example you would begin formulating your marketing campaign. You would look at how to market the shoe; you would put billboard ads in college towns, and perhaps sponsor a tennis match locally for college students who could win two pairs of these new tennis shoes in a match. This campaign is defined and formulated through marketing segmentation. Again, you would target the marketing of tennis shoes to people who plays tennis, and you found out in the research of your marketing segmentation that women are more excited about tennis then men, and college students are in the majority of those who play tennis. Based on this research, you would then market to this distinct population. You have found similarities in those who play tennis and some differences. There has to be a given amount of appropriate information or reasonable assumptions about consistency within the segments and differences between them. Market segmentation thus allows the organization to locate and tailor its offerings for one or a number of the identified segments in the marketing process.[8]

    These fancy words add value to the main rationale: You want to market your product in a way which is competitive, cost effective, creates value, and has room for a diverse market. For example, college students in Italy could buy the tennis shoes also; hence there are financial rewards in thinking globally in the 21st century. Italy, Japan, Costa Rica, Canada, Ireland, and England -- they too want to have the best and coolest tennis shoes and operationally it makes sense to look at the global market. Diversifying your marketing strategy globally, and if it makes sense to do so, will also be answered during the segmentation process.

---

[8] Tonks, 2009

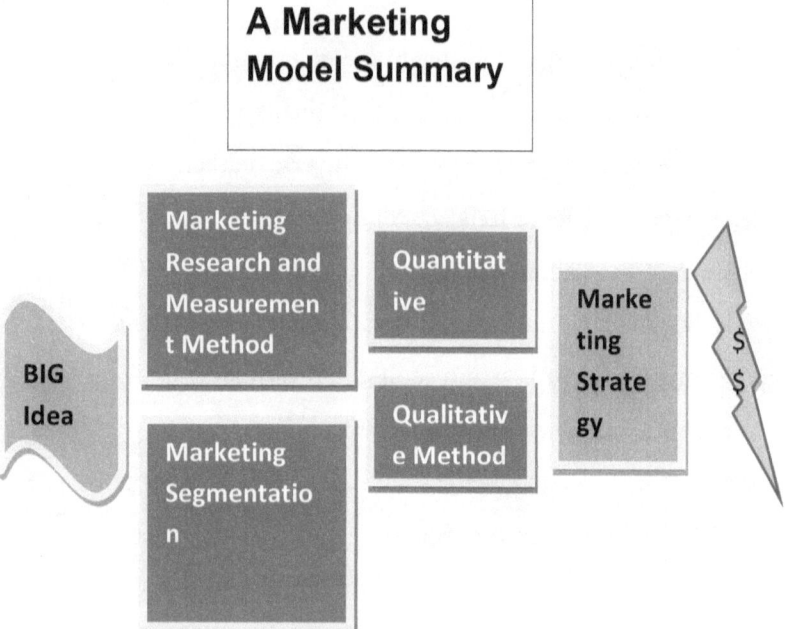

Segmentation theory and practice can be instrumental in gaining a competitive advantage. "The lack of guidance in the segmentation literature can help explain why companies have problems segmenting their market."[9] Research has a hard time trying to explain how to offer theories on how to segment your market. You have to be able to brainstorm your own marketing segmentation. What is your competitive advantage? Are your shoes the best looking shoes in the world, or are they the cheapest? Answer a simple question like this and you have begun your quest towards the marketing segmentation process. Think outside the

---

[9] Clarke, 2009, p. 346

box and then ask more and more questions until you find yourself an audience. This audience is who you will be building your marketing strategy towards. This will be your competitive advantage. You have found you are the company who has the best shoes; and now you have to find a way to narrow your audience and tell them you are the leader in the industry when it comes to shoes. This is refined marketing segmentation. Asking and answering many questions about your brand, company, product, service, is the beginning of your own marketing segmentation.

## Would You Rather a Blueberry Pie or Just Some Blueberries & Ice Cream?

Marketing segmentation is like making a pie; if made right you get a good piece of it when you are done. I am talking specifically about a piece of the market share pie. This happens only after you have planned properly and chosen a wise marketing research and measurement method and have done a good bit of marketing segmentation.

There are many different ways to carry out market segmentation. Some experts advocate a quantitative survey-based approach, using multi-dimensional approaches to identify segments. In practice, many organizations seek less radical approaches because various operational constraints affect the level of change which can be achieved.[10] "Despite ongoing interest in the notion of marketing portfolios and the emergence of portfolio management tools such as the Boston Matrix, Directional Policy Matrix, and StratPort, risk and return has received relatively little consideration in the marketing literature."[11] Within a comparison of conceptual models a discussion of evaluation, risks and benefits need to be analyzed. There are a lot of tools which can develop your marketing strategy as previously mentioned; you still have to ask the important questions.

There have been key debates in the marketing literature which note that customers are not as predictable. It is harder to pigeon hole a consumer into a specific genre; okay, you like tennis shoes, but you may also like to go to a Broadway show. Concerns that consumer lifestyles were becoming increasingly complex seem to suggest that market segmentation may thereby be less effective and efficient.[12] There will still be a lot of information you will gain from marketing segmentation. The manner, however, in which you use the information, is what determines the result. All of us can pick blueberries and eat them; most of us have sugar, and flour; just because we have these ingredients does not mean we will have a blueberry pie. Marketing segmentation is like making a pie; you have all the ingredients of information, now what do you do? Should I mix the blueberries with sugar, a touch of salt, and mix

---

[10] Dibb & Simkin, 2009
[11] Ryals, Dias, & Berger, 2007
[12] Quinn, 2009, p. 259

the flour with butter and make a crust, sounds like the recipe for a blueberry pie. Or should I just pour some sugar on the blueberries and serve them with ice cream? How you handle the information gained from the marketing segmentation is up to you; but be smart about it, and make the best result. A blueberry pie seems more appealing than blueberries and ice cream. If you have followed the proper research methods and developed a good strategy thus far, you will easily choose the right path which will get the most results. This decision will be an easy one to make.

## Big Questions, Big Answers! How about Playing "Who Wants to be a Millionaire?"

When you place your ad in Times Square, what do you want people to do? How will you measure what they do? This again is an important part of the marketing strategy and again you will need to go back to the marketing measurement methods chosen.

Once you have done your homework on marketing segmentation, the creative juices should start to flow and help you to create an original campaign. You will be able to sift through the data obtained in the segmentation process and look at your product/service differently and ultimately plan accordingly. Too many times in the past, it would be unthinkable to have a talking lizard or a dog that drove a car; it would be risky. Today, risk is rewarded with innovation and a big piece of the market, cash.

Cash is king in this type of marketing approach. Executives sitting around a conference table reviewing Excel spreadsheets are important, but not the only way of brainstorming a new marketing approach. This may have worked in the 70's and 80's where people used Lotus and looked at spreadsheets upon spreadsheets of data. Today people want to be entertained and you have to "earn" your audience. Money and value is where people find loyalty in the 21st Century. You have different generational audiences who do not think like you do, and will not think like their grandkids do either; it is your job as a marketer to be innovative and tell an interesting story to appeal to the masses while saving them cash and delivering them value for that cash. Here is the golden 21st century marketing approach as it applies to segmentation. Value is extremely important!

## Smart Begets Smart

After you have done your research and chosen a good methodology for measuring the results, now it is time to finish the marketing plan with a good and smart marketing strategy. In your marketing segmentation research, you learned about your demographic and target audiences. Who buys the products? Why? Where do they live? How old are they? Let's be simpler and more direct: Who is getting a piece of the pie (i.e. market share) and how much?

Marketing research can be the primary means by which the marketing concept is implemented. That is, marketing research is a set of procedures by which the state of want satisfaction, the *sine qua non* of marketing practice, is revealed to producers.[13] Since marketing segment analysis will give direction and provide a path for the marketing plan, integrating it into a marketing strategy will produce tremendous value.

There are limits, however, when implementing the marketing segment into a marketing strategy. In theory, marketing segmentation and marketing strategy work well side by side; the golden ticket is to marry these two.

We know a lot of guys like to drink beer during the day of the Super Bowl and have parties. The marketing segmented approach to develop strategy would go something like this: Who drinks the most beer at these parties? What sort of beer do most people drink? Men may be the answer, as might be a light or lower calorie beer. Now you have some workable answers as discovered by your marketing segmentation research. How do you develop a marketing strategy which will reach out to the men who watch the biggest football game and how do you get them to drink your new beer, Lightermister? How do you get this new beer out into the market? Since television ads for the Super Bowl are enormously expensive, do you conduct a viral marketing campaign via Facebook, Twitter and YouTube? This is how you marry the

---

[13] Saegert & Fennell, 1991, p. 262

two concepts. You know men drink the most beer at these parties. Now you have to try to develop a marketing strategy which will get those men to drink your new beer, Lightermister.

The goal of a marketing strategy is both complex and simple. The first is to become intimate with your marketing research and let it speak to you! Let this information sit with you for a bit. Your next plan of action and this will help develop a strategy which will help satisfy the desired outcome(s). From the business perspective, utilizing all resources at hand and keeping an open mind, when other internal and external forces (which we will talk about later) in the organization as well as market segmentation may influence the overall strategy, is a smart plan of action. The outcomes are now to generate your message to a new audience.

## Social Media Marketing "A Force of Nature"

There is a lot of buzz lately about social networking and how it relates to marketing strategy and is even helpful in the marketing segmentation phase. There should be a lot of buzz since social networking has transformed the way we communicate to others. However, there are confusing and conflicting statements about what social networking means in social media marketing.

Let's use LinkedIn as an example of social networking as well as how it fits into social media marketing (SMM). LinkedIn is a site where many professionals post their credentials, experience and even a profile picture. Essentially a social networking site like

Facebook, LinkedIn is similar where you are able to connect to your friends and view their connections and search for other people you may have worked with and add them to your network. There is a bigger importance here. The establishment of a LinkedIn profile is simple. It is a self-marketing tool. You build an online presence. You place a photograph, since other people who may not know your name will recognize your face. This is a lot like brand marketing. Then you link your profile with those of other professionals. Why? Not because you connect with them on a daily basis; it is because doing so creates more brand recognition to your profile on LinkedIn. People who look at your friends' profiles will now see your profile. LinkedIn *is* social media marketing. It may not be advertised as such, but it is a good example of SMM.

There are a lot of resources on social media marketing; the point here, however, is to be simple. This is brand recognition on an online scale. If you explore a few of the social networking tools such as Twitter, Facebook, LinkedIn, Ping, YouTube and interest blogs, you will find a common connection. This is people linking to other people, and other people finding out about other people; in other words, building a network or community of like-minded interests. This is social media marketing. How can this help a business? Just like building a LinkedIn profile you are creating an online presence, a recognized brand, and a network of connections.

As we discovered, SMM is about being linked to other people. Some of these people who are linked to your brand who are potential or current customers is a good way to collect data. SMM should not in of itself be used to collect data erroneously or secretly; it should be a transparent system where customers and potential customers are aware of the information you are seeking. Perhaps on your Facebook page you put a survey form or conduct a product launch test; this data can be helpful in bolstering your marketing segmentation by using social media as an outlet to obtain this information.

    The same is true with social media marketing within companies. Mostly all companies have websites. Green Oak Press, the company whom published this book, has a website (www.greenoakpress.com) While a website is an online presence, it is *not*, however, social media marketing. There is an important difference between having a website and having social marketing presence. Green Oak Press, has a Twitter account, GreenOakPress a Facebook page (www.facebook.com/GOPress, and a YouTube presence, (*John Errigo, the author*) all of these social networking sites are interconnected creating social media marketing as well as an example of how a company should utilizes social media marketing to their benefit. In addition, my company website also has a blog and links to my Twitter, Facebook and YouTube pages. You can separate them and combine them; social networking media can and should work together to get the best marketing results and creating a strong social media marketing strategy.

Social media marketing is very valuable for companies since it helps them bolster their online presence. For example, Green Oak Press, Twitter feed can "tweet" messages about upcoming events or seminars; our network of connections -- those who are following our tweets (again note the connection factor) -- will be able to instantly know about our upcoming event and may attend. Someone who may not attend our event may see our tweet and decide to follow us on Twitter and will be a candidate for a possible future event. This is the power of social marketing; *it is connecting with a broad audience and interacting with potential new customers of your product or service.* There are endless possibilities. Another vehicle for social marketing for Green Oak Press is their Facebook fan page. Seminars or teleconferences or webinars can be announced; in a Facebook post this publication and future publications will be announced. Green Oak Press Facebook page has over4 3,150 fans who "like" the page to date. Green Oak Press has fans from all over the world: USA, Indonesia, Iraq, India, Saudi Arabia, Chile, Egypt, Argentina, Costa Rica, Mexico, Japan, Canada, Nigeria and many more. The Facebook connection is an instant way to get a company message out to everyone in the whole world who is interested in Green Oak Press' activities.

The potential for SMM is unlimited. SMM can be a great tool for your marketing research; particularly marketing segmentation since you can filter out and find demographics, key markets, and (most importantly) learn about and interact with those connections who are interested in your company. Marketing segments and analysis have the same effect in the social media world. The need for segmentation of marketing research at the social networking level has extreme relevance to the overall marketing strategy and the success of the marking strategy.

Connecting all of these social media is what makes a success for your marketing strategy. Connect Twitter with YouTube, and YouTube with Facebook, and Facebook with Twitter, all of these connected facets of social networking creates a dynamic social media marketing which will get you results beyond your expectations. The key here is to keep them updated with interesting and relevant content and follow everyone in your target markets; after all, a social networking site is about being social. Use these social networking outlets as often as possible and you will be connected to more than just a new friend, a potential client, associate or the next big thing.

Social Networking is a rapidly changing medium as well as how it relates to Social Media Marketing. MySpace was once the most important social site; a few years later, along comes an unknown social networking site called "Facebook" which replaced it. No one predicted MySpace would lose its number one social networking slot; yet it happened! This is a prime example of the rapid movement and constant evolution of social networking. Be on the lookout for replacements of current social network mediums. Innovative sites such as Twitter and some social networking mediums can be replaced just as MySpace was with Facebook. Social Media Marketing's best bet for smart marketing strategy is the social networking aspect. The whole aspect of linking with other people through a variety of social networking tools together for a more dynamic impact in your overall strategy. Social networking does work and is an effective way to get your message out at little or no cost to thousands and thousands of people at light speed.

## The Force behind Marketing: What Drives Results?

When developing a marketing strategy some things never change. You still have people that actually create the strategy and those who buy or take action as a result of the strategy; these are known as external and internal forces. External forces would be the customers; internal forces would be those internally experiencing the branding of the item (such as employees, stakeholders and shareholders). Customers responding negatively to the marketing strategy would greatly help the marketing segmentation process next time around too; such reactions would also have a big influence on the marketing approach and end result. Internal and external forces have direct correlation to marketing strategies and segmentation. There is a direct link between the internal and external forces and how this link affects the actual marketing strategy. The interrelation and mutual dependence of external (customer) and internal (employee) brand experiences means they cannot be viewed as separate entities, but instead should be managed holistically. This is another new concept in the 21st century.

Just as effective external marketing is based on human resource management strategies that produce skilled and motivated marketing employees, successful internal marketing is increasingly dependent on strategies that believe employees treat consumers fairly and offer goods and services that have been sourced, promoted and distributed in socially responsible ways. It is important to note the value of the company (the brand) treating its employees just as responsibly. Reinforcement of that all-important fact was demonstrated in an article appearing in "Flack Me," a public relations professional's blog affiliated with the career site Talent Zoo. Titled "Good PR Starts Internally, Among Employees" and contributed by Doug Bedell (2011), the piece notes: "Feeling tuned-in internally helps employees feel more upbeat in functioning externally and that boosts relationships with customers." Good internal communication builds external credibility. This all might seem self-evident. Yet it's amazing how, under the stress of daily pressures, many firms neglect relating well to their own employees." How employees feel about the company that employ them (internal forces) is as big a factor as external forces which can sink or keep afloat a good marking strategy.

While marketing and public relations are different disciplines, well-toned marketing strategies can not (and should not) ignore the impact good public relations among the internal employees of an organization can have on that organization's external customer relationships and sales.

A few maxims of marketing have emerged which give clear empirical evidence of how external forces *do* affect the marketing strategy. Ethical considerations also contribute to the internal and external forces of implementing marketing segmentation and developing a marketing strategy.

The most important stakeholder is the consumer, rather than the investor, since it is the customer which the marketing strategy aims to attract. This also means making those ethical decisions to avoid embarrassment down the road. By the same token, however, the investor also has a right to expect ethical decisions since he/she has bought stock in the organization. The job of the executives, of course, is to maximize stockholder wealth. Ethical decisions do make sense for everyone; the employee, the investor, customer, and stockholder. These decisions drive results and make a marketing strategy stronger and more viable.

## Being Ethical Is Smart Strategy and Financially Rewarding

"Misleading advertising, unsafe and harmful products and abuse of channel power were already concerns in marketing fifty years ago and are still debated today."[14]

---

[14] Schlegelmilch & Oberseder, 2009, p.1

Within the context of ethics and how it relates to marketing strategy, we need to understand where the marketing has been and where it is at present. Some of the modern concerns on the effects of ethics on marketing strategy are related to "the impact of technological developments on marketing." [15]

"The term 'marketing ethics' has been defined as the systematic study of how moral standards are applied to marketing decisions." [16] Schlegelmilch & Oberseder found eighteen issues relevant to marketing ethics within their review of the literature of the past 50 years. These were identified as ethical issues concerning products themselves, pricing, placement and promotion, sales and decision making, consumers and predatory consumer practices, international and cross-cultural marketing ethics, marketing research, marketing education, social marketing, green marketing, the law, effective use of the Internet, religion, and politics. As noted, there is plenty of evidence of scholarly review of marketing and the effects of ethics and how they are interconnected.

A few ethical maxims would help illustrate this point: Do unto others as you would have them do unto you; Would I be embarrassed in front of colleagues/family/friends if the media publicized my decision?; Are there any payments that could not be fully disclosed in company accounts?; Good ethics is in the firm's

---

[15] Ibid.
[16] Op. cit.

best interest; When in doubt, don't. These maxims reveal that not only are there laws to obey, but there are also people's reputations. People's actions and decisions are oftentimes closely monitored.

Influences such as society, family, and friends (since they would be the ones most affected) could be seen as external forces compelling a marketer to be ethical and negate ethical dilemmas. "All the standard ethical prescriptions in the field of marketing can be reduced conceptually to (a) obey the law or (b) act in your own self-interest, i.e., do what is right because if you do not, it will be damaging to your interests in the long run."[17]

Societal expectations are the driving force and interconnecting link between marketing ethics and its philosophical nature. Society quickly shapes marketing strategy. If a product is being marketed and consequently viewed negatively by the public due to a grave or moral problem, it will then have an enormous impact on the organization and how it approaches its overall marketing strategy. While not directly related to the sales of its products, the 2010 oil well disaster in the Gulf of Mexico took an enormous toll on BP's organizational structure and its PR/marketing/communications strategies, not to mention shareholder anger.

For the marketer, it is important to make ethical decisions which have a concern for the customer. "A customer might decide that the advertiser is ethically motivated (i.e., wants to sell

---

[17] Gaski, 1999, p. 316

the product and simultaneously genuinely wants to help or improve the consumers situation) or is unconcerned with ethics (i.e., simply wants to sell product regardless of its effects on the consumer's life)."[18]

Besides societal and philosophical forces, there are many others which affect a marketing strategy and its overall ethics. "In marketing, the issue of ethics derives from marketing professionals' relationship with the parties in the exchange process, i.e., organizational members (superiors, peers, and subordinates), competitors, customers, and the general public."[19]

From the available research, it is clear the customer is not the only or sole factor with respects to ethical decision-making within the process to formulate and implement an effective marketing strategy. Laws, politics, obeying the shareholder's/customer's interest, how the product is branded and advertised (does the producer/marketer/advertiser have the interest of the consumer at heart, or is he just seeking to make a profit) – all these concerns fall under the umbrella of ethics. Research has shown that an overweening desire for profit which trumps ethics will tragically lead to the downfall of any marketing strategy, no matter how innovative and or cunning the strategy itself may be. Obviously, ethics is good for business, marketing strategy and starting the revolution of a new idea.

---

[18] Davis, 1994, p. 874
[19] Akaah, 1992, p. 599

## Starting the Revolution of Your "Big Idea"

Now the pieces of the marketing puzzle are coming together. Your big idea now has some definite deliverables on how to get it out onto the big stage. This booklet has set out to make the marketing concepts realistic and worthy of immediate implementation. There is first developing methodologies which would help determine the best course of research for the marketing plan in the formation stage. Evaluating the research is important in creating direction and momentum within a marketing strategy. There is inherent value in developing focus segments in the marketing strategy, in evaluating the internal and external forces within the organization in relation to the marketing plan as well as the ethical and legal implications of the plan itself. A good marketing strategy is constantly evolving, based on the methodologies chosen, the marketing segmentation research and finally the internal and external forces. A top-notch marketer will adjust and flex the plan accordingly to achieve the desired outcome without compromising the original integrity of the elements of the marketing strategy. The marketing strategy will be successful since a flexible approach in all of these areas has been maintained.

Go back to the questions on what makes you visit your favorite place, or buy your favorite product. These questions are the same questions you need to ask to start your revolutionary new idea on the global stage. What will make your product unique? As you know, there is work that needs to be done after you have a big idea. By asking the right questions in the right manner and using the information wisely, the marketing strategy you subsequently develop will give you a big yield or return. Each question asked about your big idea is a return on investment ten times the stock market average. In order to be successful you need not know everything, but you need to know *something*, and hopefully this something is knowledge of how to ask questions and make decisions about revolutionizing your big idea! Marketing know-how principles will get you there. Your big idea will now be the next phenomenon if all the ingredients are planned just right, and you use a smart marketing strategy to get you there.

    You are at the beginning of an exciting journey. Now you have the knowledge and the know-how principles of marketing to refer to and have a clearer mindset of what marketing is and what it has become. I look forward to learning about your new idea and hearing about your success instantaneously. Now, go get started!

## Index of Sources

Akaah. (1992). Social Inclusion as a Marketing Ethics Correlate. *Journal of Business Ethics*, 599-608.

Clarke, H. (2009). Business-to-Business Marketing. *Journal of Business-to-Business Marketing*, 343-373.

Davis, J. (1994). Good Ethics is Good for Business: Ethical Attributions and Response to Environmental Advertising. *Journal of Business Ethics*, 873-885.

Dibb, S., & Simkin, L. (2009). Implementation rules to bridge the theory/practice divide in market segmentation. *Journal of Marketing and Management*, 375-396.

Foedermayr, K. E., & Diamantopoulos, A. (2008). Market Segmentation in Practice: Review of Empirical Studies, Methodological Assessment, and Agenda for Future Research. *Journal of Strategic Marketing*, 223–265.

Gaski. (1999). Does Marketing Ethics Really Have Anything to Say? - A Critical Inventory of the Literature. *Journal of Business Ethics*, 315-334.

Peterson, J. (2010). Quantitative Marketing. *Economic Development Journal*, 35-41.

Quinn, L. (2009). Market segmentation in managerial practice: a qualitative examination. *Journal of Marketing and Management*, 253-272.

Robertshaw, G. (2007). Epistemological limitations in quantitative marketing research: implications for empirical generalisations. *Journal of Empirical Generalisations in Marketing Science*, 1-13.

Ryals, L., Dias, S., & Berger, M. (2007). Optimising marketing spend: return maximisation and risk minimisation in the marketing portfolio. *Journal of Marketing Management*, 991-1011.

Schlegelmilch, B. B., & Oberseder, M. (2010). Half a Century of Marketing Ethics Shifting Perspectives and emerging trends. *Journal of Business Ethics*, 1-19.

Tonks, D. G. (2009). Validity and the design of market segments. *Journal of Marketing Management*, 341-356.

www.ingramcontent.com/pod-product-compliance
Lightning Source LLC
Chambersburg PA
CBHW030516220526
45464CB00006B/2815